Study the alphabet chart. Then trace the letters.

1

Study the alphabet chart. Then trace the letters.

a b c d e f g h i j

k l m n o p q r s t

u v w x y z

a b c d e f g h i j

k l m n o p q r s t

u v w x y z

Look at the arrows. Practice writing each letter.

Direct oval letters

Upper-loop letters, direct oval

Upper-loop letters, indirect oval

Cone-stem letters

Cursive Writing

Look at the arrows. Practice writing each letter.

Compound-curve letters

Lower-loop letters

Boat-ending letters

Indirect oval letters

Look at the arrows. Practice writing each letter.

Intermediate letters

Undercurve beginnings: minimum letters

i *w* *ww* *e* *v* *s* *t* *d* *p*

Lower-loop letters

j *g* *y* *z* *f* *q*

Tick-check letters

b *o* *vw* *v* *s*

Cursive Writing

Look at the arrows. Practice writing each letter.

Undercurve beginnings: upper-loop letters

Overcurve beginnings: hump-letters

Downcurve beginnings: small oval group

Practice writing the letter. Practice writing the sentence.

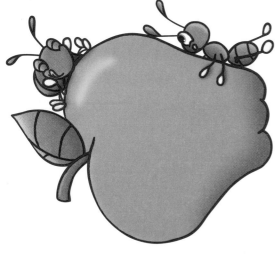

$\mathcal{A}$ $\mathcal{A}$ $\mathcal{A}$

a a a

Annie Ant ate an apple.

Practice writing the letter. Practice writing the sentence.

$\mathscr{B}$ $\mathscr{B}$ $\mathscr{B}$

ℓ ℓ ℓ

Big Bob is a brown bear.

Practice writing the letter. Practice writing the sentence.

$\mathscr{C}$ $\mathscr{C}$ $\mathscr{C}$ $\mathscr{C}$

c c c

Cool Cat collects cookies.

Practice writing the letter. Practice writing the sentence.

𝒟 𝒟 𝒟

𝒹 𝒹 𝒹

Daring Dan is a deep-sea

diver.

10

Practice writing the letter. Practice writing the sentence.

$\mathscr{E}$ $\mathscr{E}$ $\mathscr{E}$

e e e

Ed Elephant eats everything.

Practice writing the letter. Practice writing the sentence.

Fancy Fish feels funny.

Practice writing the letter. Practice writing the sentence.

𝒢 𝒢 𝒢

𝒢 𝒢 𝒢

Gail Goat likes green grass.

Practice writing the letter. Practice writing the sentence.

𝓗 𝓗 𝓗 𝓗

𝓱 𝓱 𝓱 𝓱

Happy Holly has a hat.

Practice writing the letter. Practice writing the sentence.

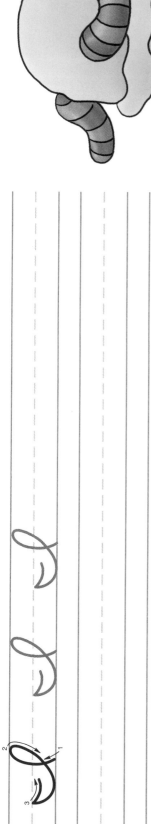

$\mathcal{I}$ $\mathcal{I}$ $\mathcal{I}$

$\mathcal{U}$ $\mathcal{U}$ $\mathcal{U}$

Iris Inchworm is in the

ice cream.

Practice writing the letter. Practice writing the sentence.

J *J* *J*

f *f* *f*

Jolly Joe juggles jelly jars.

16

Practice writing the letter. Practice writing the sentence.

$\mathcal{K}$ $\mathcal{K}$ $\mathcal{K}$

k k k

$\mathcal{K}$im $\mathcal{K}$angaroo kept the kite.

Practice writing the letter. Practice writing the sentence.

$\mathscr{L}$ $\mathscr{L}$ $\mathscr{L}$

$\mathscr{l}$ $\mathscr{l}$ $\mathscr{l}$

Larry Lion loves leaves.

Practice writing the letter. Practice writing the sentence.

$\mathcal{M}$ $\mathcal{M}$ $\mathcal{M}$ $\mathcal{M}$

m m m m

Mighty Monkey moves the

moon.

19

𝒩 𝒩 𝒩

𝓃 𝓃 𝓃

Nice Nurse needs a notebook.

Practice writing the letter. Practice writing the sentence.

Ollie Octopus occupies the ocean.

$\mathcal{P}$ $\mathcal{P}$ $\mathcal{P}$

p p p

Pink Pig plays the piano.

Practice writing the letter. Practice writing the sentence.

Q Q Q

Q Q Q

Quiet Queen quit quilting.

Practice writing the letter. Practice writing the sentence.

R R R

n n n

Rowdy Raccoon rocks the
railcar.

Cursive Writing

Practice writing the letter. Practice writing the sentence.

Silly Seal swims to school.

Practice writing the letter. Practice writing the sentence.

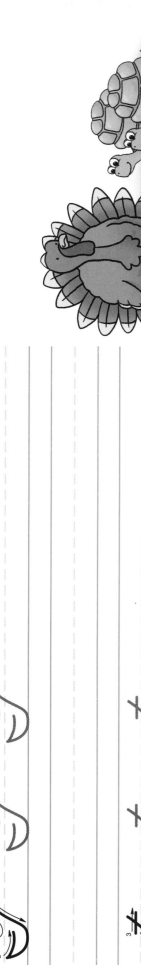

$\mathcal{T}$ $\mathcal{T}$ $\mathcal{T}$

t t t

Tom Turkey talks to two turtles.

Practice writing the letter. Practice writing the sentence.

$\mathcal{U}$ $\mathcal{U}$ $\mathcal{U}$

u u u

Uppity Umpire uses an umbrella.

Practice writing the letter. Practice writing the sentence.

𝒱 𝒱 𝒱

𝓋 𝓋 𝓋

Vera Violet has a violet vase.

28

Practice writing the letter. Practice writing the sentence.

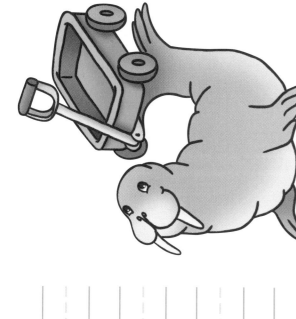

$\mathcal{W}$ $\mathcal{W}$ $\mathcal{W}$ $\mathcal{W}$

w w w

Weary Walrus wants a wagon.

Cursive Writing

Practice writing the letter. Practice writing the sentence.

𝒳 𝒳 𝒳 𝒳

𝓍 𝓍 𝓍 𝓍

Xavier X. had an extra x-ray.

Practice writing the letter. Practice writing the sentence.

$\mathcal{Y}$ $\mathcal{Y}$ $\mathcal{Y}$ $\mathcal{Y}$

y y y y

Yvette Yak yearns for a yo-yo.

Practice writing the letter. Practice writing the sentence.

Zany Zebra zigzags to the zoo.

A Authors

Write the name of the author for each book title.

| Milne, A.A. | Twain, Mark | Potter, Beatrix | Seuss, Dr. | White, E.B. |

1. The Adventures of Tom Sawyer

2. The Tale of Peter Rabbit

3. Winnie-the-Pooh

4. The Cat in the Hat

5. Charlotte's Web

Cursive Writing

B Buildings

Write the name of the building that matches each clue.

| library | school | hospital | museum | hotel |

1. where you go to be treated for health problems

2. a place that displays objects of permanent value

3. where learning takes place

4. where books may be borrowed or read

5. a building that provides lodging

C Coins

Write the name of the coin that matches each clue.

| penny | nickel | dime | quarter | half-dollar |

1. the coin with Abraham Lincoln on it

2. the coin with Thomas Jefferson on it

3. the coin with Franklin Roosevelt on it

4. the coin with George Washington on it

5. the coin with John F. Kennedy on it

       Cursive Writing

D Dogs

Write the name of the dog that matches each clue.

| husky | boxer | greyhound | pointer | beagle |

1. not a bus

2. points the way

3. rabbit chaser

4. does not wear gloves

5. looks like a wolf

E Ecosystems

Write the answer that completes each sentence.

| ecology | habitat | oxygen | meteorology | botany |

1. The environment in which a species lives is its_____.

2. _____ is the study of how plants and animals interact.

3. The study of plants is called_____.

4. _____is the science of weather.

5. Plants and animals need water and _____ to live.

F Farm Animals

Write the name of the animal that matches each clue.

sheep	horse	cow	chicken	pig

1. raised on a dairy farm

2. raised for meat on a hog farm

3. raised mainly for riding

4. raised for both food and clothing

5. raised for meat and eggs

G Board Games

Write the name of the board game that matches each clue.

| Candy Land® | Chess | Monopoly® | Clue® | Scrabble® |

1. uses play money to buy and sell real estate

2. often a child's first board game

3. a strategy game played to capture the opponent's king

4. a word game that requires spelling and vocabulary

5. a detective game

Cursive Writing

H Habitats

Write the habitat that matches each clue.

| desert | oceans | swamps | rainforests | grasslands |

1. a very dry place, not all are hot

2. wide areas covered with grasses and trees

3. hot and humid parts of the world

4. a home to fish and mammals

5. wetlands that are flooded all the time

I Insects

Write the name of the insect that matches each clue.

ladybug	firefly	mosquito	termite	ant

1. terminator

2. picnic pest

3. vampire insect

4. pyromaniac

5. female bug

J Jokes

Write the answer that makes each joke funny.

| palm | She wanted rich soil. | It gets unhoppy. | bedbugs | three days old |

1. What is an insect after it is two days old?

_____

_____

_____

2. What happens when a frog gets stuck in the mud?

_____

_____

_____

3. Why did the gardener bury her money?

_____

_____

_____

4. Which trees clap?

_____

_____

_____

5. What kind of insect sleeps most?

_____

_____

_____

K Know Your Bones

Label the bones with the correct words.

| skull | kneecap | ankle | shin | collarbone | elbow | jaw | pelvis |

1. _____

2. _____

3. _____

4. _____

5. _____

6. _____

7. _____

8. _____

L Logic Puzzles

Patti, Mary, and Paul have different favorite foods.
Read the information in the charts below to complete the puzzle.
Write each child's favorite food on the line.

Patti _____

Mary _____

Paul _____

Patti does not like chicken or pizza.

	Patti	Mary	Paul
Pizza	no		
Spaghetti	yes		
Chicken	no		

Mary will not eat foods that have tomatoes in them. (Hint: If Mary does not like foods with tomato, then she must like chicken.)

	Patti	Mary	Paul
Pizza	no	no	
Spaghetti	yes	no	
Chicken	no	yes	

Paul likes a food that starts with the same letter as his name. (Hint: If Paul likes pizza, then spaghetti or chicken must not be his favorite.)

	Patti	Mary	Paul
Pizza	no	no	yes
Spaghetti	yes	no	no
Chicken	no	yes	no

M Mammals

Write the name of the animal that matches each clue.

| whale | elephant | bat | fox | giraffe |

1. the longest neck

2. carries a trunk

3. the blue one is the largest *mammal*

4. *flying mammal*

5. known as sly

N Numbers Quiz

Solve the problems. Write the answers in the puzzle.

Across

A. 10 more than 25 = _____

B. 120 – 15 = _____

C. 51 + 35 = _____

D. 25¢ + 30¢ = _____ ¢

E. 137 – 64 = _____

F. one dozen = _____

G. 85, 90, 95, _____

H. 9 tens, 2 ones = _____

I. 6 x 8 = _____

J. 28 ÷ 2 = _____

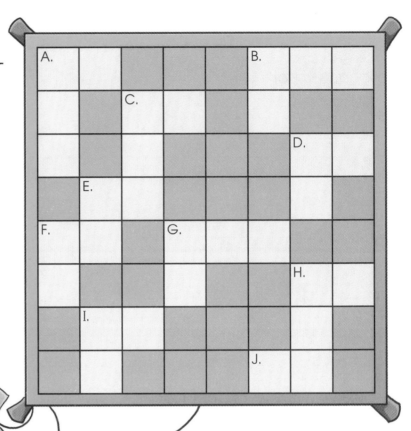

Down

A. 372 + 17 = _____

B. 2 x 9 = _____

C. 8 hundreds, 5 tens, 3 ones = _____

D. 105 – 54 = _____

E. 8 x 9 = _____

F. 4, 8, 12, _____

G. 45 ÷ 3 = _____

H. 9 hundreds, 7 tens, 4 ones = _____

I. 85¢ – 40¢ = _____ ¢

O Oceans

Write on the lines to show where each ocean is located.

| Atlantic Ocean | Indian Ocean | Pacific Ocean | Arctic Ocean | Antarctic Ocean |

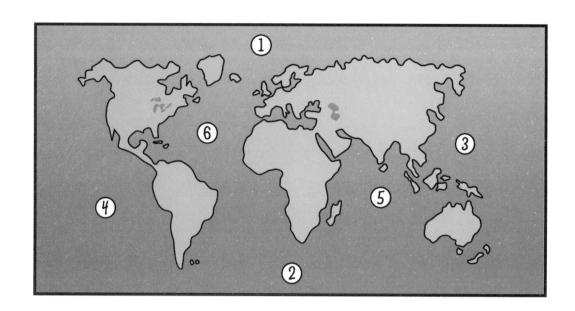

1. _____

2. _____

3. _____

4. _____

5. _____

6. _____

P Presidents

Write the name of the president who matches each clue.

Lincoln	Washington	Jefferson	Reagan	Kennedy

1. the youngest elected president

2. known as "Father of this Country"

3. a former actor who became president

4. president during the Civil War

5. was responsible for the Lewis and Clark expedition

Q Simile Quiz

The nouns are in the wrong similies. Write the correct noun on each line.

silk	bear	feather	bug	night

1. as light as a ~~rock~~

2. as dark as ~~silk~~

3. as hungry as a ~~wink~~

4. as cute as a ~~bone~~

5. as smooth as ~~night~~

R Rivers

Write where each river is located.

North America	Africa	South America	Asia

1. Nile

2. Amazon

3. Yangtze

4. Mississippi

S Sun

Write the answer that completes each sentence.

| energy | galaxy | light and heat | gas | Milky Way |

1. _____ is another word for star system.

2. The sun shines because it gives out_____ and_____.

3. A star is made of_____and has no solid surface.

4. Our galaxy is named the _____ _____.

5. Light and heat are forms of_____.

51

T Analogy Test

Write the word that completes each analogy.

computer	author	pound	rug	brake

1. Grass is to ground as _____ is to floor.

2. Bat is to baseball player as _____ is to writer.

3. Scissor is to cut as hammer is to _____.

4. Artist is to painting as _____ is to novel.

5. Engine is to go as _____ is to stop.

U United States

Write the answer that matches each clue.

| Alaska | Lake Michigan | New York | fifty | Missouri |

1. the largest lake within the U.S. borders

2. the number of states in the U.S.

3. the largest state

4. the longest river

5. the largest city

V Vegetables

Write the name of each vegetable under the correct plant part.

yam

lettuce

broccoli

bean

pea

spinach

flower
_____

cauliflower

carrot

stem
_____

celery

leaf
_____

asparagus

seed
_____

root
_____

W Weather

Write the answer that matches each clue.

| tornado | thunderstorm | hurricane | snowstorm | rainbow |

1. My favorite dance is the twist.

2. I turn everything white.

3. I'm one of the prettiest things that comes with rain.

4. I'm bigger and badder than a tornado.

5. When I rain, I pour, and pour some more.

X X Marks the Spot

Write the name of the city found at each set of coordinates.

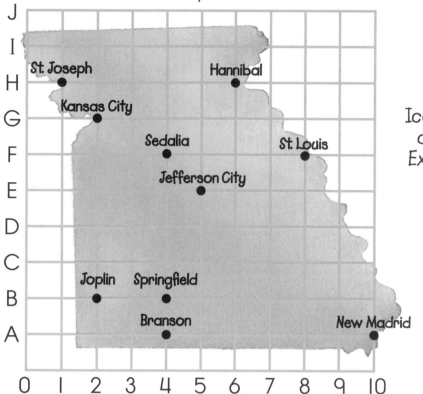

Missouri

Ice cream cones were first served at the 1904 Louisiana Purchase Exposition World's Fair in St. Louis.

1. (4,A)

2. (2,B)

3. (8,F)

4. (2,G)

5. (6,H)

6. (4,F)

Y Yellowstone Park

Write the answer that completes each sentence.

Wyoming	glaciers	Louisiana Purchase	geyser	first

1. Yellowstone Park was shaped by volcanoes and _____.

2. The Yellowstone region was acquired as part of the _____ _____.

3. Yellowstone Park is located mainly in _____.

4. Old Faithful is a famous _____ in the park.

5. Yellowstone was the _____ national park in the U.S.

Z Zoo Quiz

Write the name of the animal that matches each clue.

| platypus | flea | ostrich | cheetah | chameleon |

1. I run up to 70 miles per hour.

2. I grow up to 9 feet tall and weigh 300 pounds.

3. I can jump up to 200 times the length of my own body.

4. My tongue can be longer than the length of my body.

5. I lay eggs instead of live young.

Water Words

Write the word that matches each description.

tide	currents	salt	waves	sand

1. These are like giant rivers in the ocean.

2. something you can taste in the ocean water

3. the daily rise and fall of ocean water caused by the sun and the moon

4. These form when winds move ocean water toward the shore.

5. tiny pieces of rock and coral

Cursive Writing

Idioms

Idioms are expressions or phrases that do not mean what they say.
Match each idiom with its meaning.

| get angry | tell a secret | not understood | happy | be quiet |

1. clear as mud

2. walking on air

3. bite your tongue

4. blow your top

5. spill the beans

Leaping Lizards

Write the word that completes each sentence.

| tails | insects | iguana | tongue | dinosaurs |

1. Lizards lived during the time of the _____.

2. A chameleon catches bugs with its long, sticky _____.

3. One lizard that eats plants is the _____.

4. Some lizards eat _____.

5. Some lizards drop their _____ when they're in trouble.

Weather Words

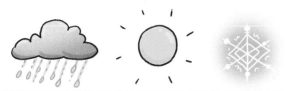

Write the word that completes each sentence.

wind	water	air pressure	precipitation	condensation

1. Rain, snow, and hail are kinds of_____.

2. Drops of water on a cold can are_____.

3. The push of air on the earth is_____ _____.

4. Cold air can't hold as much_____as warm air.

5. Moving air is_____.

Sports

Write the word that matches each clue.

| baseball | bowling | squash | golf | soccer |

1. Batter up!

2. small ball

3. not a veggie

4. tenpins

5. It's a kick!

Answer Key

Page 33
1. Twain, Mark
2. Potter, Beatrix
3. Milne, A.A.
4. Seuss, Dr.
5. White, E.B.

Page 34
1. hospital
2. museum
3. school
4. library
5. hotel

Page 35
1. penny
2. nickel
3. dime
4. quarter
5. half-dollar

Page 36
1. greyhound
2. pointer
3. beagle
4. boxer
5. husky

Page 37
1. habitat
2. Ecology
3. botany
4. Meteorology
5. oxygen

Page 38
1. cow
2. pig
3. horse
4. sheep
5. chicken

Page 39
1. Monopoly
2. Candy Land
3. Chess
4. Scrabble
5. Clue

Page 40
1. desert
2. grasslands
3. rainforests
4. oceans
5. swamps

Page 41
1. termite
2. ant
3. mosquito
4. firefly
5. ladybug

Page 42
1. three days old
2. It gets unhoppy.
3. She wanted rich soil.
4. palm
5. bedbugs

Page 43
1. skull
2. jaw
3. collarbone
4. elbow
5. pelvis
6. kneecap
7. shin
8. ankle

Page 44
spaghetti
chicken
pizza

Page 45
1. giraffe
2. elephant
3. whale
4. bat
5. fox

Page 46

A.3	5			B.1	0	5
8		C.8	6		8	
9		5		D.5	5	
	E.7	3			1	
F.1	2	G.1	0	0		
6			5		H.9	2
I.4	8				7	
	5			J.1	4	

Page 47
1. Arctic Ocean
2. Antarctic Ocean
3. Pacific Ocean
4. Pacific Ocean
5. Indian Ocean
6. Atlantic Ocean

Page 48
1. Kennedy
2. Washington
3. Reagan
4. Lincoln
5. Jefferson

Page 49
1. feather
2. night
3. bear
4. bug
5. silk

Page 50
1. Africa
2. South America
3. Asia
4. North America

Page 51
1. Galaxy
2. light and heat
3. gas
4. Milky Way
5. energy

Page 52
1. rug
2. computer
3. pound
4. author
5. brake

Page 53
1. Lake Michigan
2. fifty
3. Alaska
4. Missouri
5. New York

Page 54
flower: broccoli, cauliflower
stem: celery, asparagus
leaf: lettuce, spinach
seed: pea, bean
root: yam, carrot

Page 55
1. tornado
2. snowstorm
3. rainbow
4. hurricane
5. thunderstorm

Page 56
1. Branson
2. Joplin
3. St. Louis
4. Kansas City
5. Hannibal
6. Sedalia

Page 57
1. glaciers
2. Louisiana Purchase
3. Wyoming
4. geyser
5. first

Page 58
1. cheetah
2. ostrich
3. flea
4. chameleon
5. platypus

Page 59
1. currents
2. salt
3. tide
4. waves
5. sand

Page 60
1. not understood
2. happy
3. be quiet
4. get angry
5. tell a secret

Page 61
1. dinosaurs
2. tongue
3. iguana
4. insects
5. tails

Page 62
1. precipitation
2. condensation
3. air pressure
4. water
5. wind

Page 63
1. baseball
2. golf
3. squash
4. bowling
5. soccer